D1443704

DEC 1 4

THE BEST MLB
CATCHERS
OF ALL TIME

By Bo Smolka

Published by ABDO Publishing Company, PO Box 398166, Minneapolis, MN 55439. Copyright © 2014 by Abdo Consulting Group, Inc. International copyrights reserved in all countries. No part of this book may be reproduced in any form without written permission from the publisher. SportsZone™ is a trademark and logo of ABDO Publishing Company.

Printed in the United States of America,
North Mankato, Minnesota
092013
012014

Editor: Chrös McDougall
Series Designer: Christa Schneider

Photo credits: AP Images, cover (left), 1 (left), 7, 9, 11, 13, 15, 17, 19, 21, 25, 29, 37; Tom Olmscheid/AP Images, cover (right), 1 (right), 55; Harry Harris/AP Images, 23; Rob Burns/AP Images, 27; Harry Cabluck/ AP Images, 31; Bob Daugherty/AP Images, 33; Richard Drew/AP Images, 35; Paul Benoit/AP Images, 39; Reed Saxon/AP Images, 41, 49; Charles Krupa/AP Images, 43; Orlin Wagner/AP Images, 45; Ed Betz/AP Images, 47; Ross D. Franklin/AP Images, 51; Paul Battaglia/AP Images, 53; Brad Rempel/Icon SMI, 57; Jeff Roberson/AP Images, 59; Scott Kane/Icon SMI, 61

Library of Congress Control Number: 2013945888

Cataloging-in-Publication Data
Smolka, Bo.
 The best MLB catchers of all time / Bo Smolka.
   p. cm. -- (Major League Baseball's best ever)
Includes bibliographical references and index.
ISBN 978-1-62403-113-7
1. Major League Baseball (Organization)--Juvenile literature.   2. Catchers (Baseball)--Juvenile literature. 3. Catching (Baseball)-- Juvenile literature. I. Title.
796.357--dc23

                                                    2013945888

TABLE OF CONTENTS

INTRODUCTION

Catcher is often called the toughest position in baseball.

The catcher has to work with the pitcher on every pitch. And he has to be ready for any situation at any time. In addition, wearing all that protective gear can be tough, especially on a 95-degree day. So can being hit by foul tips and being run into by a base runner. Plus catchers crouch behind the plate more than 100 times per game, occasionally pouncing up and making a rocket-like throw. But the best Major League Baseball (MLB) catchers do all of that. Then they can also take off the gear and clobber the ball as hitters.

Here are some of the best catchers in MLB history.

GABBY HARTNETT

The Chicago Cubs and the Pittsburgh Pirates were tied in the bottom of the ninth inning. First place was on the line. And with darkness falling fast, so was the game. Chicago's Wrigley Field had no lights.

Cubs catcher Gabby Hartnett stepped up to bat. He quickly went down 0–2 in the count. That is when Harnett slammed a pitch through the darkness and into the bleachers for a home run, giving the Cubs the win.

The win put Chicago in first place in the National League (NL). The Cubs went on to win the 1938 NL pennant. Hartnett's blast became known as the "Homer in the Gloamin'." Gloamin' referred to the twilight closing in at Wrigley Field. The play was just one highlight in a career filled with them.

Gabby Hartnett was a cornerstone behind the plate for the Chicago Cubs for nearly two decades.

In 1925, Hartnett hit 24 home runs.

At the time, that was the most in one season by a catcher. Five seasons later, he hit 37. Then in 1935, Hartnett hit .344 with 91 runs batted in (RBIs). He was the NL Most Valuable Player (MVP) that season.

Hartnett played in the major leagues for 20 seasons. He helped the Cubs win four NL pennants. In 1938, he took over as manager midway through the season. With Hartnett as catcher and manager, the Cubs rallied to win the pennant.

Hartnett also had a rocket for a throwing arm. Runners who tried to steal on him often regretted it. Hartnett threw out 56 percent of runners trying to steal. Through 2013, that ranked second-best all time. Former manager Joe McCarthy once said that Hartnett "was the greatest throwing catcher that ever gunned a ball to second base."

236

The number of home runs Hartnett hit during his career. When he retired in 1941, the 232 he hit as a catcher was a record for the position.

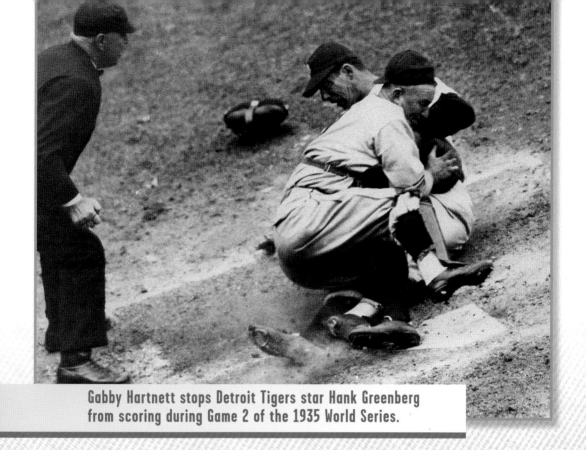
Gabby Hartnett stops Detroit Tigers star Hank Greenberg from scoring during Game 2 of the 1935 World Series.

GABBY HARTNETT

Hometown: Woonsocket, Rhode Island

Height, Weight: 6 feet 1, 195 pounds

Birth Date: December 20, 1900

Teams: Chicago Cubs (1922–40)
New York Giants (1941)

All-Star Games: 1933, 1934, 1935, 1936, 1937, 1938

MVP Award: 1935

MICKEY COCHRANE

Detroit Tigers catcher Mickey Cochrane waited on second base.

Teammate Leon "Goose" Goslin lined a single into center field. Cochrane raced around third. As fans began pouring out onto the field, Cochrane scored the winning run. The Tigers had just won the 1935 World Series. It was the first championship for Detroit.

"When I raced home with that run it was the happiest moment of my life," Cochrane said after the game.

Cochrane was not just the star catcher on that team. He also was the manager. Cochrane was one of the finest catchers of the 1920s and 1930s. He was part of a Philadelphia Athletics dynasty that won three straight American League (AL) pennants from 1929 to 1931. After the 1933 season, Cochrane was traded to the Tigers.

Mickey Cochrane was a star player and also a manager for the Detroit Tigers.

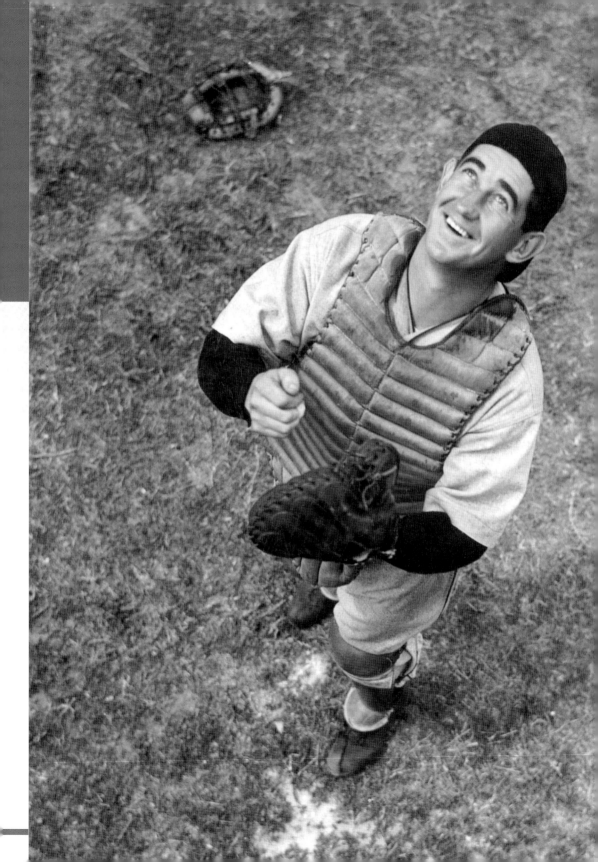

The Tigers had won 75 games the year before Cochrane arrived. In 1934, with Cochrane as catcher and manager, they won 101 games and the pennant. Cochrane hit .320 and was named the AL MVP. He was valuable off the field, too. The Great Depression of the 1930s hit Detroit especially hard. But the Tigers' success under Cochrane gave the city hope.

Cochrane had a career batting average of .320. He also was durable. He caught more than 110 games 11 seasons in a row.

Cochrane's career came to a scary end. In 1937, he was hit in the head by a pitch. Players at the time did not wear helmets. So Cochrane suffered a fractured skull. He never played again.

64

The number of triples Cochrane hit during his career. That is the most among Hall of Fame catchers that played in the twentieth century.

Tigers catcher Mickey Cochrane tags out Bill Jurges of the Chicago Cubs during Game 5 of the 1935 World Series.

MICKEY COCHRANE

Hometown: Bridgewater, Massachusetts

Height, Weight: 5 feet 10, 180 pounds

Birth Date: April 6, 1903

Teams: Philadelphia Athletics (1925–33)
   Detroit Tigers (1934–37)

All-Star Games: 1934, 1935

MVP Awards: 1928, 1934

BILL DICKEY

Bill Dickey turned on the pitch and drove it high and deep to right field. His two-run home run turned out to be the only runs in Game 5 of the 1943 World Series. And that 2–0 win gave Dickey and the New York Yankees yet another title.

The Yankees were a dynasty in the 1930s and early 1940s. They won four straight World Series titles from 1936 to 1939. And they reached the Fall Classic three times in a row from 1941 to 1943. Dickey's teammates, including Babe Ruth, Lou Gehrig, and Joe DiMaggio, grabbed more headlines. But Dickey established himself as one of the greatest catchers of all time.

Bill Dickey helped the New York Yankees win seven World Series.

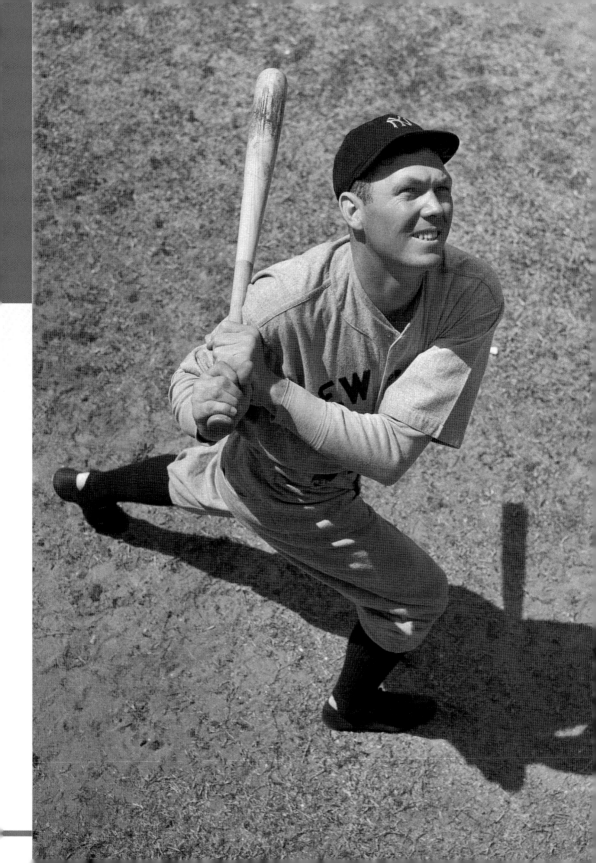

Dickey caught more than 100 games for 13 straight seasons. That had never before been done. He was a master at handling a pitching staff. He studied opposing hitters and figured out their weaknesses, which made Yankees pitchers better. That is one reason why the Yankees won more than 100 games six times with Dickey as a regular.

Dickey also produced at the plate. He drove in more than 100 runs every year from 1936 to 1939. In 1936, he hit .362. That set a record for batting average by a catcher—a record that stood for 70 years. Dickey's career batting average of .313 is still one of the best ever for a catcher.

Hall of Fame pitcher Bob Feller once said that, "Bill Dickey is the best [catcher] I ever saw. He was as good as anyone behind the plate, and better with the bat."

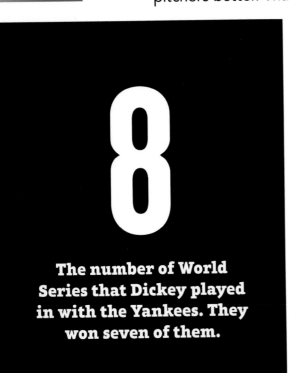

8

The number of World Series that Dickey played in with the Yankees. They won seven of them.

Yankees catcher Bill Dickey, *right*, poses with his brother George "Skeets" Dickey during spring training in 1934.

BILL DICKEY

Hometown: Bastrop, Louisiana

Height, Weight: 6 feet 1, 185 pounds

Birth Date: June 6, 1907

Team: New York Yankees (1928–43, 1946)

All-Star Games: 1933, 1934, 1936, 1937, 1938, 1939, 1940, 1941, 1942, 1943, 1946

YOGI BERRA

New York Yankees catcher Lawrence "Yogi" Berra crouched behind the plate. Pitcher Don Larsen looked in for the sign. Berra called for a pitch on the outside corner. And the pitch came right where Berra had asked for it. Strike three. The game was over.

Berra jumped up and leaped into Larsen's arms. With Berra calling the pitches, Larsen had just pitched the only perfect game in World Series history.

That was Game 5 of the 1956 World Series. Berra and the Yankees went on to win the series in seven games. That was one of 10 World Series titles for Berra with the Yankees, including five straight from 1949 to 1953. Berra played in a total of 75 World Series games during his career. Through 2013, that was a record.

New York Yankees catcher Yogi Berra grabs a foul pop during a 1962 game against the Kansas City Athletics.

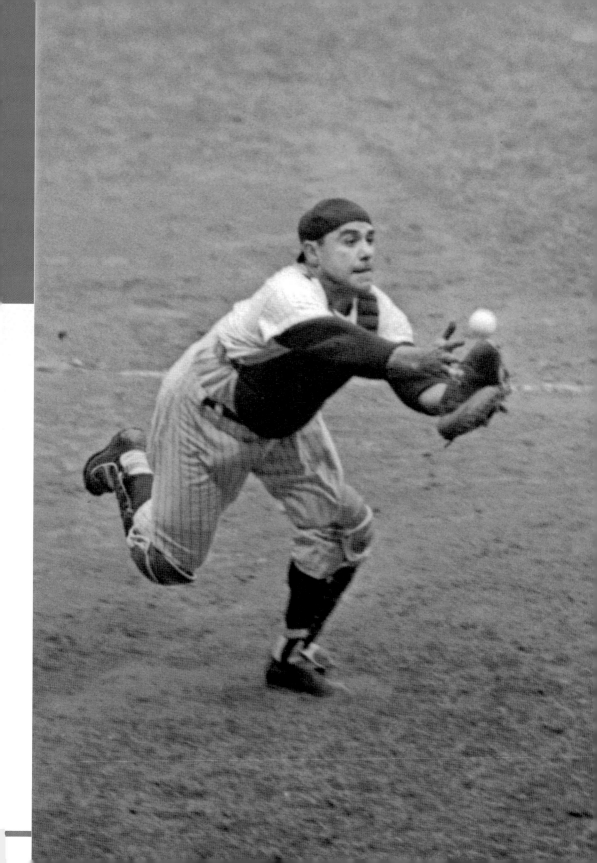

Behind every great pitching performance is a good catcher. And Berra was one of the best. He was an All-Star for 15 straight seasons. He did all the work behind the plate that a catcher is supposed to do. He studied opposing hitters. He set good targets for his pitchers. And he made strong, accurate throws.

Berra also was a force at the plate. He hit 20 or more home runs 10 seasons in a row. He also drove in more than 100 runs five times. In 1954, Berra hit .307 with 22 home runs and 125 RBIs. He was named the AL MVP that year. He again won the award the next year. Through 2013, he was still the only catcher to win a league MVP Award in two straight seasons.

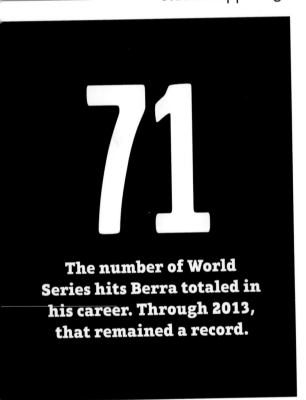

71

The number of World Series hits Berra totaled in his career. Through 2013, that remained a record.

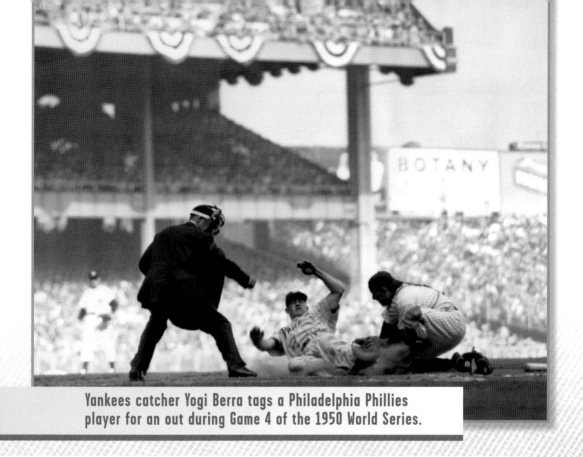

Yankees catcher Yogi Berra tags a Philadelphia Phillies player for an out during Game 4 of the 1950 World Series.

LAWRENCE "YOGI" BERRA

Hometown: St. Louis, Missouri

Height, Weight: 5 feet 7, 185 pounds

Birth Date: May 12, 1925

Teams: New York Yankees (1946–63)
New York Mets (1965)

All-Star Games: 1948, 1949, 1950, 1951, 1952,
1953, 1954, 1955, 1956, 1957, 1958, 1959,
1960, 1961, 1962

MVP Awards: 1951, 1954, 1955

ROY CAMPANELLA

Brooklyn Dodgers catcher Roy Campanella was ready. New York Yankees infielder Billy Martin took his lead at first base in the 1955 World Series. As the pitch was thrown, Martin bolted for second. Behind home plate, Campanella caught the pitch. In one motion, he pounced to his feet and fired a dart to second base. Martin was tagged out trying to steal.

In his career, Campanella threw out 57.4 percent of would-be base stealers. Through 2013, that was still a major league record. But it was not just his arm that made Campanella a Hall of Fame catcher. He also was tough as nails and a powerful hitter. He hit more than 30 home runs four times in his career. And he was named the NL MVP three times.

Roy Campanella followed Jackie Robinson to the Brooklyn Dodgers, becoming one of the first black stars in MLB.

The 1955 season might have been Campanella's best. He hit .318 with 32 home runs. Three times in the previous six years, the Dodgers had reached the World Series. They had lost to the Yankees in all of them. But 1955 was different. The Dodgers again faced the Yankees in the World Series. This time, however, Campanella hit two home runs and caught four Yankees trying to steal. And the Dodgers finally beat the Yankees in seven games to win the World Series.

Campanella began his career in the Negro Leagues. He then joined the Dodgers in 1948, one season after Jackie Robinson had broken the color barrier. Campanella quickly showed he belonged. He was an All-Star eight years in a row. But his career was cut short by an injury. Campanella was paralyzed in a car accident before the 1958 season.

40

The number of home runs Campanella hit as a catcher in 1953. That set a record for home runs by a catcher in one season. He hit 41 total homers.

The Dodgers' Roy Campanella connects with a pitch during a 1955 game.

ROY CAMPANELLA

Hometown: Philadelphia, Pennsylvania

Height, Weight: 5 feet 9, 200 pounds

Birth Date: November 19, 1921

Team: Brooklyn Dodgers (1948–57)

All-Star Games: 1949, 1950, 1951, 1952, 1953, 1954, 1955, 1956

MVP Awards: 1951, 1953, 1955

JOHNNY BENCH

Runners rarely risked trying to steal on Johnny Bench. The Cincinnati Reds' catcher could catch the pitch and fire the ball to second base in one lightning-quick motion. Few runners could beat the throw.

Bench was an offensive star for the Reds in the 1970s. But his defense might have been even better. He is considered by many to be the best catcher of all time.

With Bench behind the plate, Cincinnati rolled in the 1970s. The team was known as the "Big Red Machine." The Reds won six division titles, four pennants, and two World Series titles during that decade.

Bench's defense played a large role in his team's success.

Cincinnati Reds catcher Johnny Bench prepares to unleash a throw to second base during a 1983 game.

In the 42 playoff games he played in from 1970 to 1976, the Reds stole 50 bases. Their opponents stole only two. After a while, teams simply stopped trying to run on him.

In 1970, Bench blasted 45 home runs and racked up 148 RBIs. Both statistics led the NL, and he was named the NL MVP. In the 1976 World Series, Bench batted .533 with two home runs. He was named the series MVP as the Reds swept the New York Yankees.

Bench also changed the way the position is played. Previously, catchers used two hands to catch. Bench made catching a one-handed position. By keeping his throwing hand behind his back during a pitch, it was protected from injury on foul tips.

"I want to be remembered as the greatest catcher who ever played," Bench said near the end of his career. "I wanted that when I was 19 years old."

327

The number of home runs Bench hit as a catcher during his career. That was a record among catchers when he retired.

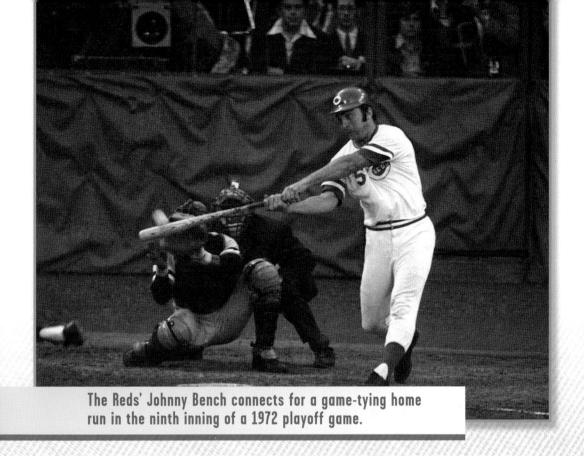

The Reds' Johnny Bench connects for a game-tying home run in the ninth inning of a 1972 playoff game.

JOHNNY BENCH

Hometown: Oklahoma City, Oklahoma

Height, Weight: 6 feet 1, 197 pounds

Birth Date: December 7, 1947

Team: Cincinnati Reds (1967–83)

All-Star Games: 1968, 1969, 1970, 1971, 1972, 1973, 1974, 1975, 1976, 1977, 1978, 1979, 1980, 1983

Gold Gloves: 1968, 1969, 1970, 1971, 1972, 1973, 1974, 1975, 1976, 1977

MVP Awards: 1970, 1972

Rookie of the Year: 1968

CARLTON FISK

Carlton Fisk dug into the batter's box.
It was the bottom of the 12th inning of Game 6 of
the 1975 World Series. Fisk's Boston Red Sox were
trailing the Cincinnati Reds three games to two. Boston
needed to win to stay alive in the series.

Fisk slammed a knee-high pitch high and deep
down the left-field line. As the ball sailed toward the
left field foul pole, Fisk began jumping up and down.
As he watched the ball, he waved both his arms to the
right as if to say, "Stay fair!"

The ball hit the pole before bouncing back onto
the field. It was a home run! The Red Sox won. The
next day they lost Game 7, but Fisk's home run showed
how important he was to his team.

Boston Red Sox catcher Carlton Fisk waves for his home run
to stay fair in Game 6 of the 1975 World Series.

That was true for years. Fisk played 24 seasons in the major leagues. Through 2013, that was the most by a catcher.

In his first full season with the Red Sox, in 1972, Fisk was named the AL Rookie of the Year. Also known as "Pudge," Fisk was an All-Star 11 times. His 351 home runs as a catcher are among the most in history.

Fisk worked just as hard behind the plate. He won the Gold Glove as a rookie. And he was great at scouting opposing batters. He learned where they liked pitches thrown. That way, he could signal to his pitchers to keep the ball away from those spots. A good pitcher usually has a good catcher to thank, and Fisk was one of the best.

25

The record number of innings Fisk caught in a 1984 game between the Chicago White Sox and the Milwaukee Brewers. The 25-inning game was played on two consecutive days.

Carlton Fisk of the Chicago White Sox chases down a Baltimore Orioles base runner during the 1983 playoffs.

CARLTON FISK

Hometown: Bellows Falls, Vermont

Height, Weight: 6 feet 3, 200 pounds

Birth Date: December 26, 1947

Teams: Boston Red Sox (1969, 1971–80)
Chicago White Sox (1981–93)

All-Star Games: 1972, 1973, 1974, 1976, 1977, 1978, 1980, 1981, 1982, 1985, 1991

Gold Glove: 1972

Silver Sluggers: 1981, 1985, 1988

Rookie of the Year: 1972

THURMAN MUNSON

The New York Yankees were trailing the Kansas City Royals in Game 3 of the 1978 AL Championship Series.
Yankees catcher Thurman Munson stepped up to the plate and blasted a mammoth home run to left-center field. That gave the Yankees a 6–5 lead. They went on to win the game, and they won the pennant the next day.

The Yankees, who had been so dominant in the 1950s, had fallen on hard times. They had not reached the postseason in 12 seasons. But Munson helped change that. He was a leader on the Yankees' teams that reached the World Series each year from 1976 to 1978.

New York Yankees closer Goose Gossage leaps into Thurman Munson's arms after winning the 1978 AL pennant.

Munson was the AL Rookie of the Year in 1970. And he was the AL MVP in 1976. For three straight years, Munson hit better than .300 and had more than 100 RBIs. Through 2013, he was one of just three catchers to do that. Munson also won three consecutive Gold Gloves in his career. Plus, he was tough and durable. He played more than 100 games at catcher for nine seasons in a row.

.373

Munson's career batting average in 16 World Series games. He was 25-for-67 with one home run and 12 RBIs.

"I like a good batting average," Munson once said. "But what I do every day behind the plate is a lot more important, because it touches so many more people and so many aspects of the game."

By the late 1970s, Munson was one of the best catchers in baseball. But his career came to a tragic end. On August 2, 1979, Munson was killed when a small plane he was piloting crashed in Ohio. He was just 32 years old.

The Yankees' Thurman Munson prepares to make a play at the plate against the California Angels in 1973.

THURMAN MUNSON

Hometown: Akron, Ohio

Height, Weight: 5 feet 11, 190 pounds

Birth Date: June 7, 1947

Team: New York Yankees (1969–79)

All-Star Games: 1971, 1973, 1974, 1975, 1976, 1977, 1978

Gold Gloves: 1973, 1974, 1975

MVP Award: 1976

Rookie of the Year: 1970

GARY CARTER

The New York Mets were down to their last out. It was Game 6 of the 1986 World Series. The Mets trailed the Boston Red Sox 5–3 in the 10th inning. Mets catcher Gary Carter stepped up to the plate. If he got out, the Mets' season would be over. However, as he did so often in his career, Carter came up big.

Carter slapped a single to left field to keep the inning alive. The next three batters also reached base, and the Mets secured a stunning 6–5 victory. They won the World Series title two days later.

Carter played for 19 major league seasons and caught 2,056 games. That was still an NL record in 2013.

New York Mets catcher Gary Carter is lifted into the air after the Mets won the 1986 World Series.

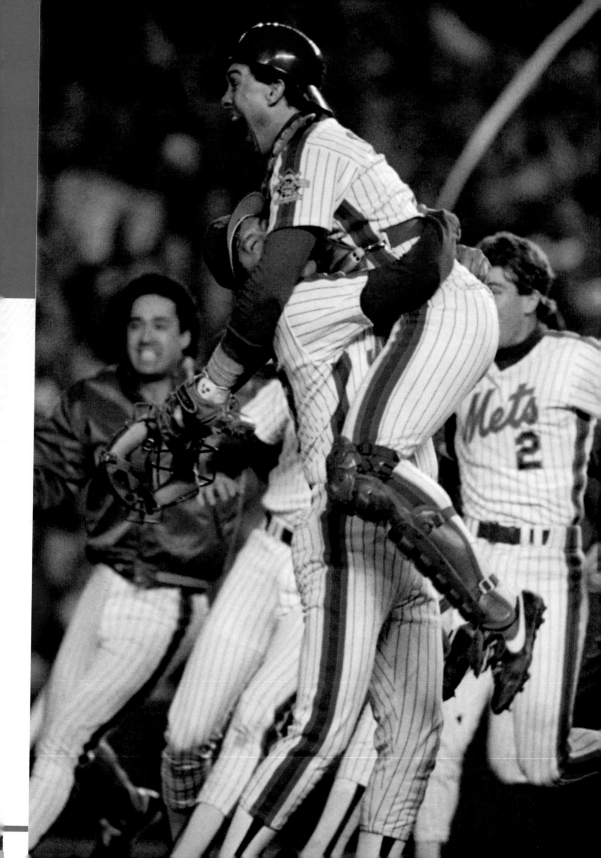

Carter was a force at the plate, with a consistent, powerful swing. And he was strong behind the plate, too. In 1983, Carter threw out 75 would-be base stealers. That year was one of the three in which he led the league in that category.

324

The number of career home runs Carter hit. He hit 298 of them as a catcher. Through 2013, that ranked sixth all time.

Carter played his first 11 seasons with the Montreal Expos. That was the first Canadian team in the major leagues, and Carter was its first superstar. Before the 1985 season, the Mets traded four players for Carter. He hit a game-winning home run in his first game for the Mets. Carter later helped the Mets to their dramatic 1986 World Series win, and he was an All-Star for 10 straight seasons.

Hall of Fame manager Dick Williams said, "Johnny Bench was the number one catcher of the '70s. Gary Carter [was] the number one catcher of the '80s."

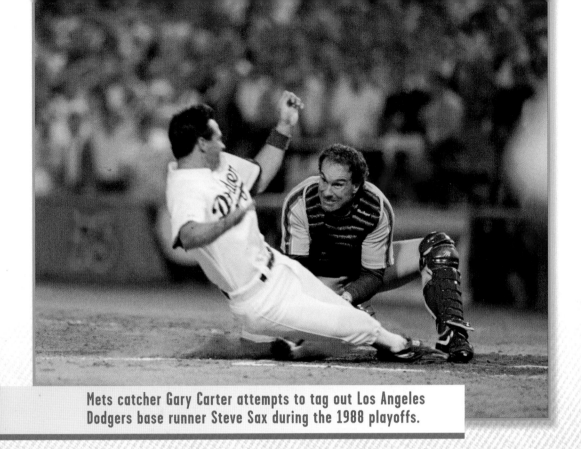

Mets catcher Gary Carter attempts to tag out Los Angeles Dodgers base runner Steve Sax during the 1988 playoffs.

GARY CARTER

Hometown: Culver City, California

Height, Weight: 6 feet 2, 205 pounds

Birth Date: April 8, 1954

Teams: Montreal Expos (1974–84, 1992)
New York Mets (1985–89)
San Francisco Giants (1990)
Los Angeles Dodgers (1991)

All-Star Games: 1975, 1979, 1980, 1981, 1982, 1983, 1984, 1985, 1986, 1987, 1988

Gold Gloves: 1980, 1981, 1982

Silver Sluggers: 1981, 1982, 1984, 1985, 1986

IVAN RODRIGUEZ

Florida Marlins catcher Ivan "Pudge" Rodriguez stood at home plate and waited for the throw from left field.

San Francisco Giants base runner J. T. Snow rounded third and sprinted toward home plate. Rodriguez caught the throw. He held the ball tight and braced for a collision. Snow lowered his shoulder and barreled into Rodriguez. Rodriguez flipped over backwards. But he held on to the ball. Snow was out. The Marlins had just won the 2003 NL Division Series.

A home plate collision is one of the toughest parts of a catcher's job. And Rodriguez was involved in plenty of them. He played 2,427 major league games at catcher. Through 2013, that was a record. Rodriguez played on six teams during his career. He helped the Texas Rangers win three divisional titles. And he won the World Series with the Marlins.

Florida Marlins catcher Ivan "Pudge" Rodriguez celebrates with the trophy after his team won the 2003 World Series.

Rodriguez, a native of Puerto Rico, reached the majors by age 19. In his second season, he won the first of his 10 straight Gold Gloves. Rodriguez made life miserable for opposing base runners. Nine times, his caught-stealing percentage led the AL.

"He had the quickest release and accuracy I've ever seen," major league manager Ron Washington said. "He was the scariest guy to have back there when you were at first base. . . . He was a special catcher."

In 1999, Rodriguez won the AL MVP Award. He batted .332 with 35 home runs, 113 RBIs, and 25 stolen bases that season. He finished his career with a .296 average and 311 home runs.

13

The number of Gold Gloves Rodriguez won. Through 2013, that was a record for a catcher. Johnny Bench is the only other catcher to have more than seven.

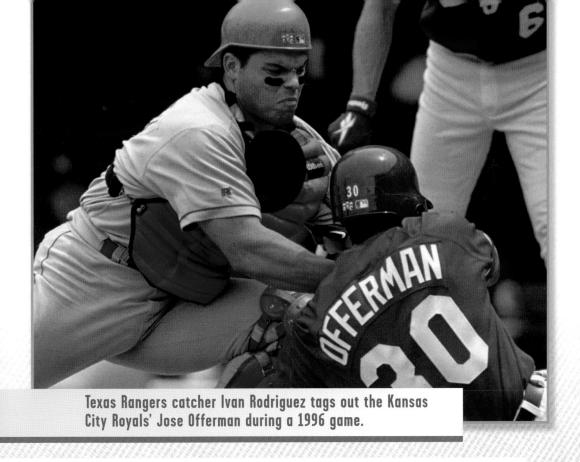

Texas Rangers catcher Ivan Rodriguez tags out the Kansas City Royals' Jose Offerman during a 1996 game.

IVAN RODRIGUEZ

Hometown: Manati, Puerto Rico

Height, Weight: 5 feet 9, 205 pounds

Birth Date: November 27, 1971

Teams: Texas Rangers (1991–2002, 2009)
Florida Marlins (2003)
Detroit Tigers (2004–08)
New York Yankees (2008)
Houston Astros (2009)
Washington Nationals (2010–11)

All-Star Games: 1992, 1993, 1994, 1995, 1996, 1997, 1998, 1999, 2000, 2001, 2004, 2005, 2006, 2007

Gold Gloves: 1992, 1993, 1994, 1995, 1996, 1997, 1998, 1999, 2000, 2001, 2004, 2006, 2007

MVP Award: 1999

Silver Sluggers: 1994, 1995, 1996, 1997, 1998, 1999, 2004

MIKE PIAZZA

New York Mets catcher Mike Piazza waited on the 3-1 pitch. Then he clobbered it. The ball flew over the fence and hit the scoreboard in right-center field at New York's Shea Stadium. Piazza had just hit his 352nd career home run. That set a record for a catcher.

And Piazza was not done. He finished his career with 396 home runs as a catcher and 427 overall. He had made his mark as the greatest power-hitting catcher of all time.

Piazza was not a superb defensive catcher. He was not the best at blocking balls or throwing out runners. But he made up for that with his bat.

New York Mets catcher Mike Piazza follows through after hitting his 352nd career home run during a 2004 game.

Piazza was an offensive force from the start. As a rookie in 1993 with the Los Angeles Dodgers, Piazza hit .318 with 35 home runs and 112 RBIs. He was named the NL Rookie of the Year. From 1996 to 2000, he drove in more than 100 runs every season. He also was an All-Star 10 years in a row.

Piazza finished his career with a .308 batting average. In 1997, he hit a career-high .362 with 40 home runs. Piazza again hit 40 home runs two years later. Through 2013, only three other catchers had hit at least 40 home runs in a season.

"He was one of those hitters who could change the game with one swing," said pitcher Tom Glavine, who was an opponent and later a teammate of Piazza. "He was certainly the greatest-hitting catcher of our time, and arguably of all time."

1,389

The number of players selected before Piazza in the 1988 draft. The Dodgers picked Piazza in the 62nd round as a favor to Piazza's father, who was a friend of Dodgers manager Tommy Lasorda.

Los Angeles Dodgers catcher Mike Piazza waits for the throw as the Chicago Cubs' Sammy Sosa slides in a 1996 game.

MIKE PIAZZA

Hometown: Norristown, Pennsylvania

Height, Weight: 6 feet 3, 200 pounds

Birth Date: September 4, 1968

Teams: Los Angeles Dodgers (1992–98)
Florida Marlins (1998)
New York Mets (1998–2005)
San Diego Padres (2006)
Oakland Athletics (2007)

All-Star Games: 1993, 1994, 1995, 1996, 1997, 1998, 1999, 2000, 2001, 2002, 2004, 2005

Silver Sluggers: 1993, 1994, 1995, 1996, 1997, 1998, 1999, 2000, 2001, 2002

JORGE POSADA

Jorge Posada had been there before. As Shane Victorino of the Philadelphia Phillies grounded out, the New York Yankees stormed the field to celebrate the 2009 World Series title. In the middle of the celebration was Posada, the catcher who helped put the Yankees back on top of the baseball world.

The Yankees had long been one of baseball's most successful teams. But they went through some lean years. That changed in the late 1990s.

In 1998, Posada's first season as a regular with the Yankees, they won 114 games. No Yankees team had ever won more. They rolled to the World Series title. That began a streak of nine straight AL East titles for the Yankees. Posada and the Yankees also won three straight World Series from 1998 to 2000.

Jorge Posada was a constant behind the plate for the New York Yankees during the late 1990s and early 2000s.

Posada, a native of Puerto Rico, started as a second baseman in the minor leagues. But soon he made the transition to full-time catcher. He grew to become an outstanding catcher and an emotional leader of the Yankees.

Those Yankees teams were loaded with talent. With so many superstars, Posada was, at times, overlooked. But he was a consistent, durable player. He played for 17 seasons and in more than 1,800 career games.

Posada was excellent at handling a pitching staff. A switch-hitter, Posada hit 20 or more home runs eight times. He was a five-time All-Star. Through 2013, Posada was one of just five catchers in major league history with at least 1,500 hits, 350 doubles, 275 home runs, and 1,000 RBIs.

6

The number of World Series in which Posada played. The Yankees won four of those series.

The Yankees' Jorge Posada drives in a run during a 2010 playoff game against the Minnesota Twins.

JORGE POSADA

Hometown: Santurce, Puerto Rico
Height, Weight: 6 feet 2, 215 pounds
Birth Date: August 17, 1971
Team: New York Yankees (1995–2011)
All-Star Games: 2000, 2001, 2002, 2003, 2007
Silver Sluggers: 2000, 2001, 2002, 2003, 2007

JOE MAUER

After all 162 games of the 2009 season, the Minnesota Twins and the Detroit Tigers were tied atop the AL Central. So they played a one-game playoff to decide the division title. After 12 thrilling innings, the host Twins came out on top. The home crowd was in a frenzy. At the heart of the celebration, soaking in the roar of the crowd, was the hometown hero: Twins catcher Joe Mauer.

Mauer had grown up just a few short miles from the Twins' stadium. The team picked him first in the 2001 draft. The Twins had endured a streak of eight straight losing seasons. They finally broke that streak in 2001. Mauer broke into the lineup full time in 2005. For the next six years the Twins were among the best teams in baseball. The local legend was a big reason why.

Minnesota Twins catcher Joe Mauer guards the plate in a game against the Detroit Tigers in 2009.

Mauer reached the major leagues before his twenty-first birthday and hit .308 that season. In 2006, he hit .347 and won the AL batting title. The Twins also won the division that year. Mauer won another batting title in 2008. Then in 2009, he had a historic season. Mauer hit .365 with 28 home runs. Through 2013, that was the highest batting average ever by a major league catcher. Mauer was named the AL MVP. He also won the Gold Glove that year.

At 6 feet 5 inches, Mauer is one of the tallest catchers in history. Some people thought his height would be a problem at a position that requires playing so low to the ground. While Mauer has had knee and back problems, so have a lot of catchers. And in 2013, at age 30, he remained one of the best in the game.

3

The number of batting titles Mauer won through 2013. He was the first AL catcher to win a batting title.

The Twins' Joe Mauer is known as one of baseball's most fundamentally sound hitters.

JOE MAUER

Hometown: St. Paul, Minnesota

Height, Weight: 6 feet 5, 230 pounds

Birth Date: April 19, 1983

Team: Minnesota Twins (2004–)

All-Star Games: 2006, 2008, 2009, 2010, 2012, 2013

Gold Gloves: 2008, 2009, 2010

MVP Award: 2009

Silver Sluggers: 2006, 2008, 2009, 2010

YADIER MOLINA

St. Louis Cardinals catcher Yadier Molina crouched behind the plate and waited for the pitch. Out of the corner of his eye, he glanced at the runner on first. The batter swung and missed. Molina saw the runner take one extra step toward second base. From his knees, Molina snapped a quick throw down to the first baseman. The startled runner tried to dive back to the base, but he was too late. Molina had another pickoff.

In the early 2010s, Molina was the best defensive catcher in baseball. He beautifully blocked balls in the dirt. He pounced out of his crouch to field pop-ups and grounders. He was a master at framing pitches. And base runners feared him. Three times from 2005 to 2010, Molina led the NL in caught-stealing percentage.

St. Louis Cardinals catcher Yadier Molina prepares to whip a throw to first base against the Milwaukee Brewers in 2010.

As with Johnny Bench, teams eventually just stopped trying to run on Molina. Runners took small leads, afraid Molina would catch them napping and pick them off.

In 2012, Molina won his fifth straight NL Gold Glove. With Molina behind the plate, the Cardinals were regulars in the playoffs. In his first 10 seasons, the Cardinals reached the postseason seven times. Molina could hold his own at bat, as well. He hit .319 with 80 RBIs in 2013 and had 22 home runs in 2012.

For Molina, catching runs in the family. Molina's brothers Bengie and Jose were also major league catchers.

When asked about Yadier Molina, Cardinals pitcher Adam Wainwright said, "There's guys who bring different elements of the game, guys with more power and more speed. There's not a better catcher."

48

The number of runners Molina picked off from 2004 to 2013. That was the highest total in the majors during that span.

The Cardinals' Yadier Molina attempts to tag out Pittsburgh Pirates base runner Brandon Inge during a 2013 game.

YADIER MOLINA

Hometown: Bayamon, Puerto Rico

Height, Weight: 5 feet 11, 220 pounds

Birth Date: July 13, 1982

Team: St. Louis Cardinals (2004–)

All-Star Games: 2009, 2010, 2011, 2012, 2013

Gold Gloves: 2008, 2009, 2010, 2011, 2012

HONORABLE MENTIONS

Bob Boone – Boone's 2,225 major league games as a catcher ranked third all time as of 2013. He hit .254 and won seven Gold Gloves from 1972 to 1990, mostly with the Philadelphia Phillies.

Roger Bresnahan – A Hall of Famer, Bresnahan was considered one of the best catchers of the early 1900s. He played with the New York Giants and others, and he also is credited with inventing catchers' shin guards.

Bill Freehan – Freehan was a mainstay with the Detroit Tigers during the 1960s. He was an 11-time All-Star and a five-time Gold Glove winner in a 15-year major league career.

Josh Gibson – Although he was not allowed to play in the MLB because he was black, Gibson arguably was the best hitter in the Negro Leagues during his career in the 1930s and 1940s.

Elston Howard – Howard was part of the New York Yankees dynasty of the 1950s and 1960s. He was selected to nine All-Star Games and was the AL MVP in 1963. In 1955, he became the first black player to play for the Yankees.

Ernie Lombardi – Lombardi was a two-time NL batting champion. He won the NL MVP Award in 1938 while with the Cincinnati Reds. He was a seven-time All-Star, and he is a Hall of Famer.

Al Lopez – Lopez caught 1,918 games in his major league career spent between four teams. That was a record when he retired in 1947. He was a two-time All-Star and, later, a Hall of Fame manager.

Lance Parrish – One of the best power-hitting catchers of the 1980s, Parrish hit 324 career home runs. He was an eight-time All-Star, three-time Gold Glove winner, and six-time Silver Slugger winner, mostly while with the Detroit Tigers.

Jim Sundberg – Sundberg's total of six Gold Gloves ranked fourth all-time among catchers through 2013. Sundberg played most of his 16-year career with the Texas Rangers and was an All-Star three times between 1974 and 1984.

GLOSSARY

draft
A system used by professional sports leagues to spread new talent among all of the teams.

dynasty
A team that wins several championships over a short period of time.

framing
The art of catching a pitch and then moving the glove quickly over the strike zone and holding it there. The goal is to try to show the umpire that a borderline pitch was a strike.

pennant
A long, triangular flag. In baseball, the word is used to describe a league championship.

perfect game
A game in which the pitcher retires all 27 of the opposing players in order, allowing no base runners.

rookie
A first-year player in the major leagues.

switch-hitter
A batter who can hit from either side of the plate.

FOR MORE INFORMATION

Further Readings

Mayne, Brent. *The Art of Catching: The Secrets and Techniques of Baseball's Most Demanding Position.* Costa Mesa, CA: Cleanline Books, 2008.

Sports Illustrated Kids. *Sports Illustrated Kids Full Count: Top 10 Lists of Everything in Baseball.* New York: Time Home Entertainment Inc., 2012.

Web Links

To learn more about MLB's best catchers, visit ABDO Publishing Company online at **www.abdopublishing.com**. Web sites about MLB's best catchers are featured on our Book Links page. These links are routinely monitored and updated to provide the most current information available.

INDEX

ABOUT THE AUTHOR

Bo Smolka is a former sports copy editor at the *Baltimore Sun* and former sports information director at Bucknell University, his alma mater. He has won several national writing awards, including the National Story of the Year from the College Sports Information Directors of America. He lives in Baltimore, Maryland, with his wife and two children. When he is not writing baseball books, he can often be found coaching his son's baseball teams.